In the Presence of Absence

In the Presence of Absence

poems

Richard Widerkehr

MoonPathPress

Copyright © 2017 Richard Widerkehr

All rights reserved. No part of this publication may be reproduced distributed or transmitted in any form or by any means whatsoever without written permission from the publisher, except in the case of brief excerpts for critical reviews and articles. All inquiries should be addressed to MoonPath Press.

Poetry

ISBN 978-1-936657-30-8

Cover art: "Morning Fog"

Oil on canvas, 36" x 48"

by Elizabeth Reutlinger

of Port Townsend, WA

Author photo: by Anita K. Boyle

Design: Tonya Namura using Liberation Serif + Avenir

MoonPath Press is dedicated to publishing the finest poets of the U.S. Pacific Northwest.

MoonPath Press

PO Box 445

Tillamook, OR 97141

MoonPathPress@gmail.com

http://MoonPathPress.com

Acknowledgments

The Bridge: "Levittown, New York"

Clover, A Literary Rag: "Balance," "Annual Report," "My Mother's Speech Therapist Asks, *Does She Speak a Foreign Language?*"

Cirque: "Allegiance"

Crack the Spine: "'Water Is Your Friend,' Said the Doctor"

Floating Bridge Review: "Wager"

Gravel: "Pear Trees on Irving Street"

Grey Sparrow: "Breath," "Picking Blueberries by a Driveway"

Jeopardy: "Counsel," "Other Clefs"

Mud Season Review: "Seeds"

Naugatuck River Review: "This Fifteenth Rib"

Northwind Poets Anthology 2013: "Not A Shrine," "Slow Curtains," "At Playa Catalonia"

Peace Poems, Volume Two: "Sun Coming Out of Cloud Cover"

Pennine Ink: "Discreet"

Poetry Quarterly: "Blue Maraca," "In the Sky"

Poetry Super Highway: "Pulling the Stopper," "Saying the Mourner's Kaddish," "Plucking Flowers"

Rattle: "In the Presence of Absence"

Rockhurst Review: "Her Practice"

Sediments: "Bitten"

Soundings: "Waiting"

Sue C. Boynton 2017 Poetry Contest Winners: "At Akumal," "What Have I Asked For?"

Sweet Tree Review: "Day Without Words"

"Saying the Mourner's Kaddish" won second prize in *Poetry Super Highway's* 2014 contest and *Clay Bird Review* reprinted it. *Noisy Water: Poetry From Whatcom County* reprinted "My Mother's Speech Therapist Asks, Does She Speak a Foreign Language?" *Sediments* and *Cirque* reprinted "Blue Maraca."

The following poems are forthcoming: "A Street Falls Upward," "Medieval Steps," "Lunch," "Days Like Forever," and "In My Life" will appear in *Avatar,* and "Like Bees and Sunlight" in *Nomad's Choir Poetry Review.* World Enough Writers will reprint "At Playa Catalonia" in the forthcoming Beer, Wine, and Spirits Poems Anthology, and *The Binnacle* will print "A Street Falls Upward."

I want to thank poets who helped with this manuscript: Gayle Kaune, Patricia Hooper, George Such, Karen Seashore, Jim Bertolino, Karen Vande Bossche, and Jay Klokker. I want to thank the Madrona Writers whom I worked and sang with during residencies at Centrum: Tom Aslin, Dianne Butler, Teri Cohlene, Janet Cox, Michael and Toni Hanner, Jordan Hartt, Gayle Kaune, Jenifer Lawrence, Ellie Mathews, Bob McFarlane, Bonnie Nelson, Don Roberts, Sam Roxas-Chua, Karen Seashore, Diana Taylor, David Thornbrugh, and Carl Youngmann. Gayle gave us the prompt, "Not A Shrine," and led exercises where I wrote drafts of "This Fifteenth Rib" and "Water Is Your Friend." Ellie led a workshop where I wrote my draft of "In the Presence of Absence." I want to thank the Centrum Foundation for these residencies at Fort Worden.

Special thanks to Gayle Kaune who picked the arrangement of poems in part two and read these poems over the years. My book's title comes from John Updike's *Self-Consciousness.* It was Roby Blecker who, in an anecdote at Torah study, said, *I'm not with you, but you're with me.* The line *Death is the mother of beauty* is by Wallace Stevens. My thanks to Elizabeth Reutlinger for her lovely cover image, to Lorraine Healy for checking my Spanish phrases, and to Lana Hechtman Ayers for bringing this book to light.

Most of all, I want to thank Linda Ford for bringing love, fun, and a bit of order into my life.

Dedicated to the memory of my father and mother

and for Linda, always

Table of Contents

Counsel	3

I

Not a Shrine	7
At Playa Catalonia	8
Slow Curtains	10
Breath	12
Levittown, New York	13
Annual Report	14
Wager	16
In the Presence of Absence	17
Pulling the Stopper	20
Water Is Your Friend, Said the Doctor	21
Day Without Words	22
Bitten	23
Seeds	25
Allegiance	26
Sun Coming Out of Cloud Cover	27
Saying the Mourner's Kaddish	28
Waiting	29
Pear Trees on Irving Street	30

II

Blue Maraca	33
At Akumal: Plan B, Same as Plan A	36
Her Practice	37

The Parasails	38
Other Clefs	39
What Runs Toward Us	40
Plucking Flowers	41
What Have I Asked For?	43
This Fifteenth Rib	45
A Street Falls Upward: On Returning a Rental Car in Orlando, Florida	47
In My Life	49
Lunch	51
Medieval Steps	53
My Mother's Speech Therapist Asks, *Does She Speak a Foreign Language?*	55
Days Like Forever	58
Like Bees and Sunlight	59
Balance	60
Color Blind	61
In the Sky	62
Aerialists	63
Discreet	65
Picking Blueberries by a Driveway	66
Salt	67
At Akumal	68
About the Author	71

In the Presence of Absence

Counsel

Low in the sky, a gibbous moon
touches our road, our red house.
Black and abstract, fir trees
keep their counsel.

Some nights the stubby needles
mutter under their breaths:
Thumbprint of your father,
soft voice of your mother.

I

Not a Shrine
for my father

Take his medal for Military Merit,
I tell myself, put it next to
his Jules Jorgenson watch,

his mechanical pencil
with the picture of a woman
in a tight black dress—

she strips down to a white slip
when you turn the pencil
upside down.

Take his hat with the plastic rain cover,
put it on a shelf in your closet
next to his shoe trees.

Take that voice on the cell phone
as we raced down I-5:
I have some bad news.

File it under a month with no days.
Take old journals, photos, three wool coats,
two paintings he left you.

Say he'd have been glad you did this.
Like the woman on his mechanical pencil,
I'm upside down. Unlike her, I'm naked.

At Playa Catalonia

Chefs with white hats tall as China Line ships...
Heaven's like that on the *playa,* girls in bikinis,
as my mother says, One string above,

one below. Why do they bother? Here
everyone's GPS is turned off. No maps,
paths that go nowhere. It's possible to fall

in love over and over, without the pain
of being young. Linda isn't jealous.
After lunch, we bask as frigate birds

glide high like spiritual advisors
so deep in their mystique they won't tell us
which restaurant to eat in. In Tulum,

Mayans sacrificed in the Temple
of the Wind. Now we take a left,
a right. Music sifts through palm fronds,

fanning themselves. Small posts
throw dim light on our path. Coatis,
rodents with tails and an attitude,

beg outside the buffet, grub for bugs,
climb into the jungle. Heaven's
like that—how did we get here?

I sip my margarita. Two palm trees
bump and grind under moonlit clouds—
unearthly, yes. At dawn, waves of aqua

and lime-green say, *Forget, forget.*
Dark blue, farther out—maybe
we came from it, maybe not.

Slow Curtains

Thirst cells
in my abdomen
stake ancient claims.

Picture the pale worms,
citizens of no country,
paying my body

such attention.
I no longer ate in bakeries.
I had a biopsy in April,

and the light that afternoon
was a mouth.
The tongue, a root.

The teeth, a rake.
The dead, such as you,
streamed around me, Father.

Not ghosts. I couldn't see them.
In the exam room,
white curtains shifted.

I was in a play,
and the doctor, on cue,
said, *It's positive.*

My soul said,
*I want gray seals
doing somersaults.*

Cells chanted
their arrogant song—
this fact, that fact.

And the truth?
This red plum of grief,
that purple one of regret.

A pulse, whose pulse?
Mine or yours?
I put all my money in a sink.

Please, not these sleeves,
this dust and sunlight
in your arms.

Breath

The sky's rows and furrows,
your breath on my neck—

a gust lifts the grasses,
and they breathe.

Light runs through them
like a wind, saying, *Wind*.

Levittown, New York

Yes, we used to go by Levittown.
They'd put the place there after the war,
miles of tract homes that we didn't call
little boxes. Back then, Levittown
reminded me of the reservoir,
sunshine on housetops, row on row.
I thought of the low spray of fountains,
a fine mist rising through sun dazzle.
Seen from the hill where the parkway curved,
Levittown wavered in the heat haze,
as if there could be places
nostalgic for us, or for all the things
that hadn't happened yet.
One time my father said, *You asked
about the reservoir.* A fact, those
fountains. With a vague swipe, he nudged
poems from the edge of my dresser,
said something about my handwriting,
how wayward it was. He said,
They do it to aerate the water. For a second,
I hung above what he said, stuck
on *wayward*. I liked knowing things,
was hooked on what we called *true facts*.
The best kind were scientific facts.
They do it to aerate the water?
I liked knowing the same people who
built Levittown were tousling air
into our water, so we could breathe easy.
See, back then there were these places—
Massapequa, Valley Stream, Rye, New Rochelle—
we passed quickly, going somewhere else.

Annual Report

Spring sends me its prospectus,
apple blossoms we mistook
for hawthorns, their white froth,

a moment's self-forgetfulness.
An eagle lifts a black cat,
dead on the road. Sometimes,

when I write, I lose track of time.
My assets—what? Dregs of nostalgia,
my body a pyramid scheme,

owing a debt that's come due.
A coyote jounces like a deer,
vague in the twilight.

Last night I woke at three a.m.,
chest pounding. As a boy,
I built paper planes, armadas,

stood on the footbridge.
A smoggy king and queen
ruled the blue air, the Empire State

and Chrysler buildings.
I skated under the black sky
of a city park, ran bases

on an empty baseball diamond,
and slid into home plate,
as if it were the bottom of the ninth.

I didn't expect a biopic
this week, or a biopsy, either.
When Giuliani got surgery,

didn't run for senator,
you said, *He could've won*,
Father. I said, *He had cancer.*

So what? you replied.
I breathe in Linda's plum trees.
Outside our apartment building

in Forest Hills, we had a maple tree.
Each fall, I sat on my windowsill,
took in the new car models,

memorized their upswept fins,
read *The Kid from Tompkinsville*,
punched my baseball mitt,

and muttered corny dedications
to outfielders who'd crashed
into walls, learned to pitch

with their *other* arm.
I must jump through some hoops
and knives?

Can do, says my voice
to the nurse, as if making a wager
on *Jeopardy.*

Wager

Perhaps, I might put in a good word for skin,
at least in theory. As for the spoils,
maybe, in the next life, sin will just be sin
and won't be scourged by sips of cod-liver oil.
I'll wager, give me sixty-one more years,
and I'll burn, a Roman candle, way past lust,
write odes to myopic Jewish racketeers,
who die for a rigid code. God won't trust
my oaths, chock-full of lies, a few truths
mixed in like ballast with the bullshit. A balloon
man, he calls out to Dorothy who's ruthless.
She throws Toto onto the set of *High Noon*,
where I weep for Gary Cooper who fights alone,
till his pale bride pulls the trigger, turns to stone.

In the Presence of Absence

When I woke from anesthesia,
I was quoting Shakespeare, saying, *I feel strange,*

but, as Shakespeare says, I must greet it as a stranger.
The nurse in the recovery room

tried to orient me, but I replied, *So I have heard,
and do in part believe.* I said something

about Love Pantry, next to a Thai restaurant,
where Linda and I had joked about going.

There she was beside me. I kept saying,
So glad to see you, as if I'd come back

from the other world, casting off dread
like an anchor. I know nothing

about heaving an anchor. I know a few things
about meteors and grief. And if I'd chosen

to go on in my pedantic, loopy way,
I could've said, quoting Shakespeare,

Ruin hath taught me thus to ruminate.
But I was happy as I sucked at the ice chips

Linda fed me with a blue plastic spoon.
They were the best thing I ever tasted. At midnight,

the nurse let me have a cup of raspberry Jello.
It was the best thing I ever tasted.

If only these opiates could last, each breath not empty,
each moment bright and flickering.

When the lab tests came back,
the surgeon said, *We got the cancer.*

It hasn't spread.
Again, I felt gratitude and thirst,

which I tried to remember as the pain began,
an anchor dragging, my works and days

connected to a catheter. As I turned to my routines,
walks and one book, I tried to get it back,

that strange gift from the other side. I wanted
to join it to an orange on a white plate,

bitter at first, sweet underneath, a crow
on a picnic table, an empty bowl

that a friend filled with water for her regal white dog.
I tried to connect the crow's

arrogant croaking to the pain in my back.
But, no, you don't need to know how OxyContin

knocked the pain down from a seven to a two,
don't need to hear how they stitched me together.

On the beach at Moclips, where we went
before the surgery, Linda flew a blue kite,

a smile of pure delight on her face,
the sun half-hidden in gray-white clouds.

She said, *Maybe, this isn't the last goodbye—*
maybe you'll get lucky again.

And her face in the recovery room,
her smile—you can take a blackboard

and set God's stars on it. You can take
an orange and chew the pulp,

savor the juice that tastes like nothing else,
as the word *orange* rhymes with nothing else.

I can't tell you what Linda means to me.
Perhaps, our life isn't a string of moments,

each one no more or less important
than another, as the Buddhist poet implied.

But I was talking about gratitude and thirst.
I get to park my ancient green Subaru

under the linden trees, near the privet hedges,
with their sweet white flowers.

Pulling the Stopper

What my doctor didn't tell me was the day after surgery, when the opiates were starting to wear off, some other man in a white coat would traipse into my hospital room at six a.m., turn on the fluorescent lights, and ask, *How are we doing?* With a confident smile, he warned me, *This is gonna hurt, but it's got to happen.* With one pull, lickety-split, like a weight lifter doing a clean jerk, he plucked a bulb out of my side, as if ripping a stopper from a tub. A bladder had been inserted in the left side of my abdomen to soak up blood. Yesterday, I swam under anesthesia, felt joy when I woke and saw Linda's face. Now a stranger tore some second heart out of my side, just to show me my first one could go on beating.

Water Is Your Friend, Said the Doctor

I wonder what he cut and where,
the surgeon at his console,
guiding the sacred robotics.

Once, I saw dozens of baby sharks,
washed up on a beach near Tampa.
I didn't ever want to meet their mothers.

I want to make a picture,
so I can remember
these empty parade grounds,

the crow on the picnic table, croaking to its acolytes,
the sweet pea flowers climbing the hillside
like new members of an old *shul*.

Water is your friend, said the doctor,
but I *knew* that, landlocked, in love with these bluffs
and white ferries,

floating like apparitions,
calling me back to a circle of friends,
an orange-headed finch, and the smell of privet hedges.

As for my surgeon,
who held his breath and cut
what had to be cut,

he saved my life.
I touch the small black stone of gratitude
and start this poem.

Day Without Words

None of my words
is an alder
half-stripped of leaves.

A small plane
banks low and loud
over the fields.

White clouds,
volumes no one's opened,
blank as vellum.

Bitten

There are two ways to die in the desert,
says a barmaid with almond eyes.
*The first is to let a coral snake wrap itself
around a knot in your spine.*

It seems I've been bitten.
I try to tie off the bite
with Linda's green scarf, but can't reach
the small of my back.

The snake says, *Each to his own.*
In heaven, it's twilight, and the new arrivals
amble up the stone path to a glimmering buffet.
Don't go back, says a man who tilts his glasses

up on his head. Wind rattles
in the palm leaves, an incarnation
of some other song.
Thanks for coming, says my mother.

A thin man offers a mint from a tin box
marked Last Supper Dinner Mints.
I'm Jewish, I say. The slim-hipped barmaid
offers me a blue quilt. She reminds me

of the girl who played I'll-show-you-mine-
if-you'll-show-me-yours when we were kids.
Even though I'm in heaven, I remember
the snake and the man who sicced the snake

on me, after I tried to save him from drowning.
How was he drowning in a desert?
Was that how I died? Must I forgive him?
Just this morning, I climbed the stairs,

walked through a valley with no stones,
but there are stones in my mouth
when I sing the *Shema, Hear, O Israel.*
There's a sea of aqua and lime-green.

Girls in string bikinis lip-sync Broadway songs.
Frigate birds with narrow, V-shaped wings
soar in the upper echelons,
surely more blessed.

The light on the sea
has turned to dime-store bling struck
into a million pieces,
sun like a burning wind.

I'm in a gray terminal, a train station,
near a sign that says *Retorno.*
Another sign on the second floor
says *Sala De Espera.*

Is that the Room of Hope? I ask.
No, says a black-haired woman,
who sounds familiar. *It's the waiting room.
Most people don't want to go back.*

Seeds

The sun on lattices of dandelion fluff—
you snag a stalk that's different, one dark
clump at its tip. You strip the sheath,
inspecting wisps, brown filaments.
Look, you say, as if you've touched
the struts of other suns.
In our hawthorn tree, bees whir
like ventilators. The tree burns and hums,
as the bees crawl into white blossoms,
culling tufts of pollen they put in gold sacks
on their thighs.

Allegiance
for my father

1

June's wide-open flowers, women pushing strollers—
I think of the sun-warmed bench
where we sat, discussing foreign trade.

At a table near the farmers market,
two protestors against "Apartheid In Israel"
pass out cream-colored leaflets.

Once, you kept your voice low
as you said, *Hate is hate,
no matter how the words cry peace.*

2

It's time to make my statement
about how certain stars float in the night.

When I stand and say *Kaddish* for you,
one small black stone
becomes eternal, turning like the sea,
which takes no prisoners, and I become stubborn
as the stars,
white-hot as you were, hopeful as the foliage
of forgotten Aprils, and I know each seed
vows allegiance, each cell of my body,
each strand of DNA.

Perhaps, we'll meet
ten thousand leagues beneath my breath.

Sun Coming Out of Cloud Cover

Light on the road
runs toward me, as if lips
of wind might touch me.

I turn as this light plummets,
one green-gold cleft
on the hills.

Saying the Mourner's Kaddish
for my father

Perhaps, there's a place where songs,
as they're sung, come true—
where leaves in the elms

that once held themselves steady
sway under a streetlight,
dazed by the heat of summer.

Or there's a living room
where the thrust and parry of his talk—
where the air, choked by the smoke

of his Chesterfields, hangs heavy,
where his armchair, his chessboard,
his *Wall Street Journal* receive their blessing,

the same way the *minyan*
stands when we say *Kaddish*,
as if blessing were both call

and answer—streetlight, elm;
armchair, star—till the chess pieces
say they're through.

Waiting

The sun, half-hidden, touches the hills.
I wait for you in sums that won't come right,
black trees reflected in a roadside puddle.

Yellow leaves, each one a witness—
perhaps, your winter won't be long or white.
The sun, half-hidden, touches the hills.

Black-eyed Susans, their lattices of stamens
stand up, not asking for the light,
black trees reflected in a roadside puddle.

A fountain fills itself. I stand and listen—
cities burned with fire, your face one last time,
a sun, half-hidden, touching the hills.

It won't add up. My hands can't find your number—
spaces between stars, that song, *The Water Is Wide*,
black trees reflected in a roadside puddle.

I'm not with you, but you're with me—this cup,
this crust...Father, if you sleep, sleep tight—
black trees reflected in a roadside puddle,
the sun, half-hidden, touches the hills.

Pear Trees on Irving Street

They float, these white trees—
a few petals, fallen
to the street, not stars fading,
not snow.

The trees have blossomed
in a freezing east wind.
None, I think, has any regrets
or choice.

If the night frost
comes too thick,
too fast, they'll give
what they have to,

as if it were nothing—
these clusters,
held not by black branches,
but their own buoyancy.

II

Blue Maraca

1

Not a stone, not a rope,
but a musical note, all notes,
Mother—the first, the last
song we sang.

2

It beat time
on a beach south of Cancun
by a lime-green sea.
Linda bought it for you.

3

Music can be
a blue maraca,
if it wants to
shimmy its hips.

4

Sure, death can shake
its rattle with a bony hand,
the same hand
you pointed at me.

5

It can't be black or white.
It's blue—the way the sea
turned dark farther out,
blue darkening.

6

Can it float? Your blue
maraca might slip
away, not even
the rasp of your breath.

7

What's around it?
Some books on Linda's
cedar chest. At night
it dreams—an old crone's
fingers, her plainsong—
a girl from Yonkers,
her *patois*.

8

Blue maraca, blue maraca,
why do I...?

9

What song beat inside
you before the craftsman
took you for his gourd?
What does the word
guerdon mean?

10

I pick up your blue maraca,
and we glide
by that lime-green sea,
arms outspread.

11

What sound? No rattle,
no rictus, but joy—
a salt shaker released,
salt laughing.

12

This blue maraca,
made of lacquered wood—
you shook it like a question
with your one good hand.
Where did the air
go when you went?

At Akumal: Plan B, Same as Plan A

To sweep clouds from the streets,
to pluck the strings of *música*,
to ferry the Blue Tangs to shelter,
to guard the gecko's crevice,
to weed the spiky acres of the sun,
to smile at young couples
nuzzling in the *Sala De Espera*,
to let the breakers sift in
at night from the other world,
to gather the broken cobbles.

Her Practice

We've come back from a walk
under crumpled, white clouds—a dowry, those sails?
You fold our sheets,
pinch one billowing corner,
press east against west,
shake a sea of wrinkles out,
tucking and folding, just so.

A mystery—I can't know
how you do this, as if without
trying. Our fitted sheets, a test
for me, you fold and tuck, quarter
and halve, till the layers beneath
lie flat. Linen breakers, crinkled sails
lie stacked. On your table, white flowers, tall stalks.

The Parasails

Agoutis are invisible. Xplora tours cost too much.
Each day, the parasails glide by, these blue
archangels. Questions have no answers here,
though people keep on asking. Frigate birds float,
disembodied. A little girl names an iguana
Maxwell. He crouches in the sun, head up, waiting.
Uncles sit inert, smoking in the bar. One says
My right hip tells me it's gonna rain. Miss Akumal
teaches salsa dancing. *One, two, three....HIP.*
You suggest I join her. The wind hauls stage sets
of cumulous clouds toward Africa. You and your
sister count the days and at night forget them. Blue
parasails pull the sand mermaid into the sky.

Other Clefs
    [we play *The New World Symphony* for my
    mother in her coma]

Some bodies, quick as birds—their spirits
dance in bright air, their lives, plain as eyesight.
You filled the feeders, took the compost out,
not questioning day, or asking why night's night.
We who crave images can picture elms
where birds flit, nestling in clefts, and leaves tout
leafy theorems, what grief may be. Today,
our red maple glints. The bird feeder sways.

Perhaps, your music plays on other clefs,
in other rooms. We held your hands
as once you stroked my eyes. The sleeves
of sleep, Mother....I left. You went.
A sparrow's blue, insouciant sky, but different.

What Runs Toward Us

The sun, a funnel
on the water, its tip at the shore—
we walk on a back road
past pallet boards

and Drano cans. You spot a catbird
in low bushes.
It's going, neener, neener,
we say, laughing.

Gray-white clouds roll in—
a glint of light on gray water.
Lose the Drano cans, these clouds
could be sails

for Saint Christopher Columbus.
You point to—a wren?
A yellowthroat? Its head black and white,
body black and gray.

This is where I saw the Blue Grosbeak,
you say, as clouds open.
The sun on the water runs toward us
faster and faster.

Plucking Flowers

1

In the E.R. on your gurney,
you ask, *Is this real?*
You don't
recognize Olga,

who's cared for you
three years.
You push us away,
throw urine-soaked sheets

across the room.
*I keep seeing her face
inside a vase,*
you say.

You laugh
when she asks,
*Do you believe in God
or evolution?*

2

You sleep two nights,
two days, then sit up,
plucking flowers

from the air. *What do
you see?* I ask.
I see God, you reply.

3 A Week Later, You Come Home

We let you sleep,
sleep being just sleep,
not a ghost

antithesis to breath.
My eyes rest
on my sister's portrait.

4 You Saw God, You Said

You wince and ask,
I said that? I remember

the ambulance door closing.
I was losing everything.

5 Your Doctor Asks, *Can We Put A Feeding Tube In?*

I drive home at midnight—
moonlit clouds race by,
a gray-white scroll.
Something behind the sky
hides its face in beauty.
I hate beauty. *Why don't you*
show your face? I shout,
my voice, a raven's croak.
Next morning, you sit up.
God's right here, you say.
Did I pierce the night
for one second—my cry
more faithful than prayer?

What Have I Asked For?

Yesterday, the water tossed me
on the reef,
jarring my back, scraping

my right wrist.
Don't fall out of the ocean,
says Linda.

I line up a break
in the coral
with the fifth thatched shed.

Lying on my back,
held by waves,
sea held by blue sky,

sky held by the earth,
and the universe—
it's held by what?

    *

I'm standing
in the green shallows—
whomp,

something
hits the water
hard like prop wash.

Wings thrash.
A brown pelican's
next to me.

The thing has a bill
big as a thigh bone
that opens and closes.

This Fifteenth Rib

I've been dealt happiness,
grief, and two wild cards—
the sternum of my love,
a monolith by day,
ice pick by night.
When you died,
I said *Damn* and wept.
I must've thought
you'd keep pushing
Linda's hand away.
My second wild card's
a diagram, ropes of red
muscle, braided, the atypical
ribs of memory, lichen green,
a dead moss green.

Once, you said, *Ask her
if she wants to play.*
We dug in the mud
with our shovels
at low tide. *You two
played beautifully,*
you said. Sometimes,
I've sensed you telling me,
*It's enough. You sang
on my porch. It's enough.*
I was out of your room
when you died. Sometimes,
it happens like that. Linda's
putting out birdseed
for the towhees.

The man and woman who took
your body away
resembled two wax figures
with caked-on makeup.
The funeral director
explained it costs two
hundred dollars for a box
in which your body
would be burned. *You can
get free boxes at Safeway,*
I thought. Forgive me.
Sometimes, I pat the cat,
ask her about her day.
She tells me, and I never
get it. In Akumal, brown men
in white shirts and shorts
swept the halls, served us
coffee, called us *amigo*.
We paid them money. Yes,
I fell out of the sea. Perhaps,
there's this fifteenth rib,
moments like this, two horns,
no dilemma. There's the sea,
the sensation of being rocked
by something intimate,
dismissive—an old woman,
pointing one finger,
digging past the sternum
into the rib cage of her son.

A Street Falls Upward: On Returning a Rental Car in Orlando, Florida
a sestina

Stay with me, Mom, as I truck our bags on wheels tonight.
I'm trying to find a way out of this fenced Hertz lot
    where yellow buses
shuttle the Gold Club members to their rewards.
Driver, where's the exit? Where's the street?
A kid at a car wash gave us directions to Edith's hospital.
The manager at IHOP told us how to get back on the
    turnpike.

Now we're lost. Again. When we found the Florida
    Turnpike,
signs kept saying, *SeaWorld, Tonight's the Night.*
Edith greeted us with a mechanical chicken. The hospital
was waiting. We didn't know. These buses
have steps too tall for you. I'm trying to find the street
where the Country Inn said they'd pick us up. The rewards

of trudging on must be—what? The wards,
her flowers, her mockingbirds. We got off the turnpike
last week...Edith's snapshots, our street
from the fifties. We sang, *Tonight, Tonight.*
I'm *trying* to get us out of here. The buses
only go to the airport. What was the name of her hospital?

We never thought she'd die. Before the hospital,
didn't Edith call me *Tootsie-poo*? My reward,
you hugged her as she cried. Light breeze, bussing
us. Balsamic air. We sang *Yellow Bird* into the night.
How you filled her birdbaths after she died. A spike
in me, as you sat by your sister's body. A street

hid a parking lot. Glass walls across the street,
the West Marion Community Hospital.
The charge nurse: *Your aunt's in a better place.* The night
doc: *It had spread throughout her body*. Words
must need us to be their secrets. Tomorrow, a turnpike
will take us on a shuttle bus

to a runway where a Hawaiian princess floats on the tail
    of an Airbus.
We'll step on the moving walkway. On this street,
we're kids on a Ferris wheel, singing *Gypsies In Yon
    Wood*. A turnpike's
for naughty girls who disobey. How the hospital
held Edith just two hours till her heart said *Stop*. Our
    reward's
this wistful Hispanic driver who lifts us out of the night.

A street falls upward, a hospital,
a turnpike of suitcases on wheels. Our almost empty bus
breathes lightly. At the Country Inn, one last reward, a
    kiss goodbye at night.

In My Life

A star reassembles its shards,
as if that song were you
and me, Mother. *Can you
take care of me?* you asked.
I said *What?* Your face
sagged on one side.

Now Linda and I take you
for a drive. You sing *Born Free*.
A stone blossoms, and memory
releases its blue balloon
into a sky that gets wider and wider.
Two months ago, you lay,

doing speech therapy, chanting,
Dee, dah, duh, aay, eeh, aah,
your guttural voice like something
from *The Exorcist*. How you tried
to slow down ninety years.
I tried, too, thinking, *Death*

isn't the mother of beauty.
You are. Dinners you cooked,
pants you tapered and pressed,
times you took us swimming
at London Terrace—they're
like headlights streaming by

on this freeway. I keep trying
to catch one lost word, *April,*
as this ghost wave, cars and semis,
breaks over my head—a steady
rolling song of tar, emeralds,
Jones Beach, a scorched shirt

on your ironing board, July,
leaves stunned by streetlights—
the smell of asphalt, your far-off
gaze. You ask me to sing
that Beatles song—you call them
The Four Boys—and I do.

Lunch

Three pelicans, ministerial,
glide over green water. One
has gray stripes under its wings.

A grandmother in a black bikini
folds both hands under her belly,
as if content. Mr. Akumal

asks if I want to play bocce ball
in two minutes. White clouds
on the horizon like stage sets.

No, I'll float with the *tortugas,*
the green turtles browsing
on sea grasses.

They lift their necks
and fan themselves up
to breathe. Two remoras sway,

attached to one turtle's belly.
I float past cities—their green fans
and blue-gray branches,

knobs and shoulders of coral.
Goatfish stream by me.
Off to my left, I catch a flash—

something big, silver-gray.
I beat my fins, part the shoal
of fish with my fingers,

get out of there. Later, I learn
the Great Barracuda herds small-fry
in a circle, till it's ready.

Medieval Steps

Let's go look at the stars,
says Linda. We walk on a ledge—
black water sliding, waves unsheathing
themselves. A few stars. *I don't
like precipices,* I say.

It's not a precipice.
Something mischievous
in her grin. The white breakers
on black rocks, each spotlit crest
slow as an out-breath.

What's the opposite of fear—
black water, ancient as grace?
I've started climbing the medieval
steps at the end
of middle age, but so what?

A few hours ago, golden girls
and boys clinked glasses and clicked shutters
at the sunset, as if they were explorers,
and maybe they were,
their lawn green as Astroturf,

women in evening gowns,
guys in T-shirts and shorts, no one
throwing girls in swimming pools
as on Gatsby's lawn.
Here we had valet parking,

no limos. Pink-orange
sky, soft air. One guy snapped
pictures with his black Leica,
as if it were a kaleidoscope.
A blonde woman in a coral dress,

one hip thrust out, posed
as if making up her portfolio.
You liked hot babes back then,
said Linda, smiling. Yellow-white clouds
open. Somewhere, monk seals

poke up green-gray snouts. Black eyes.
Animate souls. On our sidewalk,
the woman in coral tips us a slight smile—
black water, still a few stars
as we pass by.

My Mother's Speech Therapist Asks, *Does She Speak a Foreign Language?*

Now, after this third stroke, though your hand
points to the towhee at your feeder,
each word has a shape, but not a name—
syllables from the Urals, scorched
valleys from the Rhur, vowels
from Romania, who knows where?
Each phoneme with its own tone,
inflection, gesture. Your finger
keeps pointing at me. Rivers.
Why don't I get it? Rock faces
past the snow line where stunted trees
chant a prayer of blood and thistles.
It's time to harvest darkness, each vowel
with as much meaning as a flower—
the vulgate of these petals,
purple-magenta, like the clematis
on Linda's trellis—some with curling
stamens, in their own vernacular.
Some other tones, perhaps, are lemon
lilies, star-shaped, rising, falling
like arias, or like chanting
Haftarah tropes. Your life,
a swag of buds and sepals,
scrolls of rhododendron.

You've always had us stop
your wheelchair as you gaze
at flowers. Linda
loves to hear yellowthroats'
whichetty, whichetty. You love
the white-crowned sparrows,

chickadees a squirrel or Stellar's jay
chases off. Your voice is you
and not you. I know you aren't
someone else. You just can't
say what you want to,
and then, out of nowhere:
You're a good man.
Off you go, cantilevered
over some green river.
I want to hear my sister
tell me how you put
peanuts in the feeder, hoping for eagles,
though it's all confused. *Things happen,
and you're not the same anymore,*
said Chloe, and you can't
tell me her story, how you
took care of her. What about
your hand that fell from the steering
wheel? I listen to your music
as if tied to a mast.

I've fallen in love with you,
though I always flinch when
you tell me to tuck in my shirt
or my voice needs training
in the lower register. And don't
I want to learn to sing opera?
It's come to this. I miss your telling
me to behave myself, though lately
I've made a game of it and told
you to behave yourself, too.
Watch out for cars, you said.
Eat your vegetables, I replied.
Now your voice is all register.

The words have left the room,
but the room keeps breathing,
and I'm the container trying to
contain...Your hand points from
your feeder to what? There must be
blue-black waves beneath a cliff,
and what's beneath the waves?
This life's the only life, you said.
When you had that second
stroke and saw the small birds,
you reached up, plucking
what? I must be true
to your story. I can't tell it
one spoonful at a time.

Days Like Forever

Miss Akumal plays volleyball on the beach.
Wearing blue shorts and a silver tank top,
she crouches, knees bent slightly, big hips
and buttocks. Her stance reminds me
of a black belt in karate. Bill catches me staring.
You're busted, he says, grinning, then adds
Hermoso culo, which means *nice butt*.
He asks, *Can you believe my sister?*
Getting in a taxi with her thermos of brandy
and her cold-ass omelette. He shakes his head,
smiles as if rueful. The water's almost colorless
beneath a cloud, the same blue-gray
of Miss Akumal's eyes, which glance
at you from Asia, or farther than that.
The sun appears to stand still.

Like Bees and Sunlight

When I look at this sheet
of paper, I see each breath
we let out, a white space,
a silence, my father
on his deathbed, my own
left hand. A few white hairs
curl on my index finger.
I see my mother, who speaks

in a murmur like bees
and sunlight, as I help her
walk with the quad cane.
One, two...I count
up to twenty-seven, till she
says, *That's enough.* Yes,
enough. When I look
at the paper, I'm standing

on the seventh step,
taking my seventy
millionth breath, steadying
my mother's gait belt.
As I lock the rubber wheels
of her wheelchair,
she sits down and asks,
Where do we go from here?

Balance

Palm fronds rattle, fancy dancers.
Brown men wearing white
clear our glasses away.

I wonder how much they're paid,
you say. In the shallows,
a pelican steps over a wave.

Remember when I used ani
in a Scrabble game? you ask
and show me a groove-billed ani

in your bird book. Each low wave,
in sequence, makes a shushing sound.
Remember when I got a seven-letter

word, entreat, *and I said,* "I entreat you
to forgive me." Waves touch the reef,
as if brushing a sleeve. A tern

holds its wings out. How can it shear
and balance? Last night, we watched
the low breakers. *They're almost*

disembodied, you said. The tern
dives, hits the water's heart.
White clouds get bigger as I write.

Color Blind

Spirea's pink I see, and stars,
those cold flamethrowers.

Fireweed, on spindly stalks,
I see as blue, not lavender.

I must have a defective gene,
for I can't see you, Mother.

Your voice on the answering
machine—I play it, yes.

Pachelbel's eight chords—major,
minor—perhaps, you sing

them with the saints, who aren't
marching. Or you listen

to the notes of prime numbers,
whose formula Dad said

no one's found. Is he waving
from across his field?

I play your message, *Hi,
it's Mom. I'll call you later.*

In the Sky

You were the river
bank that crumbled
as I sang.

Now I live in the sky.

The hills with their hackles
fade in mist.

You were the fir trees,
their necessary
disbelief—

they could never
stop trying
to pierce the sun.

No cipher can mimic
chlorophyll, breathing in,
breathing out,

no defibrillators needed,
please.

When I sang
Here Comes the Sun, you said
I brought the sun.

You gathered lobelias,
lemon lilies.

How can brown rivers
breathe?

Aerialists

When I couldn't crawl out of the sea,
waves knocked me flat.
Facedown in sand, I turned
my head and breathed.

My mother's urn has found its place
on the gate-leg mahogany
table she left us.
When I sang *The Water Is Wide*,

she gripped my index finger.
And when she couldn't speak,
she kissed my hand. Touch and go,
she was the aerialist—

so strong her grasp, sometimes
I feared she'd pull me
into the next world. I haven't
tucked her ashes in earth,

piled dirt on her urn.
Now Linda and I drive
to the lookout. Sea and sky
blend, no horizon,

just a blue abyss
shot through with white,
the knife cliffs, folded
almost in half—

ochre, black—
eroded spires
and terraces.
When I stepped

back from the drop off,
something in me
wanted to end
this search—

the sky, its blue
suffused with wonder,
yes, and sunlight
on scalloped ridges.

Discreet

When I was sick of the guile of windows,
the weariness of doors, the promises
I couldn't keep, you offered me a mantel
and a hearth, real work to do.
Doors became doors. Some windows
don't have to be looked into.

Like peony buds, knit up,
you had me with your premises,
different from streets, begging to be streets—
your strength, like lacework,
your laughter, the surface of a lake.
When fire dismantled me, you were discreet.

Picking Blueberries by a Driveway

Thimbles the color of dusk—
we roll the berries between
thumb and forefinger,
easing them into plastic
buckets, a clump in one hand,
swollen berries in the other.
The shrunken mummy berries
we toss. Ducking my head
into branches, I clutch
one stem, pull it to me.
The hum of bees in sedum
in the garden, blue-white sky—
we work our way through
afternoon, as you did,
Mother. Green stems
we bend toward us—
clasps unfasten. Clouds
of ninety summers...Berries
come off in our hands.

Salt

We searched for a salt machine
at the bottom of the sea.
Picking up shells, putting them
down was our salary.

Skies, palatial...Now
we wait for the green flash
at the end of day. Yellow
and white goatfish

float like phosphor.
As we go to sleep, days pass.
Sand castles in the sky
collapse like commodities.

Night pours from its salt
shaker, deep in streets
of rain. We need salt,
just a bit, to keep going.

At Akumal

An iguana in dry grass
tilts its green head to the sun
and basks, waiting for an insect.
It makes me happy, says Linda.
Now she's snorkeling,

and I sit on our porch.
The undersides of palm leaves
in the sun—shadows slant
across our red tile floor.
Lines in my notebook,

the lines of our railing—
I picture Linda, kicking her legs,
floating over purple knobs
of coral, as the sea turtles
fan themselves up to breathe.

I get my mask and fins.
Impassive, the iguana waits
in sunlit grass. Low breakers
meet like a seam, spill over,
unfold from the reef.

About the Author

Richard Widerkehr earned his M.A. from Columbia University and won two Hopwood first prizes for poetry at the University of Michigan. He has two collections of poems: *The Way Home* (Plain View Press) and *Her Story of Fire* (Egress Studio Press), along with two chapbooks. Tarragon Books published his novel, *Sedimental Journey*, about a geologist in love with a fictional character. He won first prize for a short story at the Pacific Northwest Writers' Conference, three awards in the Bridge's poetry contests, and two Sue Boynton Contest awards. He's held residencies at Centrum in Port Townsend, WA, and taught workshops there.

Recent work has appeared in *Rattle, Arts & Letters, Bellevue Literary Review, Floating Bridge Review, Gravel, Naugatuck River Review, Sweet Tree Review, West Trade Review,* and *Cirque*. Other poems are forthcoming in *Measure, Chiron Review, The Binnacle, Avatar,* and *Mud Season Review*. He's worked as a writing teacher in the Upward Bound Program at Western Washington University and, later, as a case manager with the mentally ill. He and his partner Linda live in Bellingham, WA.

www.ingramcontent.com/pod-product-compliance
Lightning Source LLC
Chambersburg PA
CBHW021447080526
44588CB00009B/737